The Theory of Everything

The Theory of Everything

by Josie Kearns

Mayapple Press 2009

Published by MAYAPPLE PRESS
408 N. Lincoln St.
Bay City, MI 48708
www.mayapplepress.com

ISBN 978-0932412-74-4

ACKNOWLEDGMENTS

Gecko and Firefly, Reading Physics, Eating a Star, The Number of Apples, Secret Doors: *Poetry Northwest.* Tomatoes, Water Witching: *Passages North.* Cold Blue: *The Iowa Review.* Magic Realism: *Magic Realism.* Vampires at the Laundromat: *Grimoirie.* The Planets Line Up: *Science 85, Songs From Unsung Worlds.* Satellite Father: *Boomer Girls.* Agreeing With Everyone: *Contemporary Michigan Poetry: Poems from the Third Coast.* Effects of Alcohol: *The Green Review.* Exotic: *The MacGuffin.* Inventions, Double Existence: *The MacGuffin* and garnered the first place prize in the Poet Hunt Contest. Moving Furniture: *Are You Experienced?* Template: *The Driftwood Review.* Love and Plutonium: *The Detroit News.* Period: *The Georgia Review.* Ghost Father: *Crosscurrent* special issue *Award Winners.*

I would also like to thank the following for their unyielding support and care during the years these poems were written: The Ragdale Foundation including Susan Tillett, Regin Igloria, Sylvia Browne, and Jack Dansch. She also thanks the following for their support, editing and ideas: Joseph Matuzak, Deanne Lundin, Richard Brandt, Suzanne Brodie, and David Sosnowski who will probably not read this. All have overwhelmingly helped these poems come to fruition as well as my mother-in-law, Mary Matuzak, Andrea Beauchamp, Thomas Lynch, Diane Wakoski, Vie Vee Francis, Richard Tillinghast, Pam Gemin (an extraordinary editor and poet), Linda Nemec Foster, Judith Minty (also an extraordinary editor and poet), Judith Kerman, Alice Fulton, Laura Berman, Vaughn Marlowe, Virginia Chase Sutton, Donald Hall, Thylias Moss, Philip Levine, Keith Taylor, Lorna Goodison, Robert Bixby, David Wagoner, Stephen Corey and all those who toil with writers and literature and, posthumously, my first editor, Herbert Scott.

Cover art by Audrey Niffenegger. Cover designed by Judith Kerman. Book designed and typeset by Amee Schmidt with titles in Copperplate Gothic Light and text in Californian FB.

Contents

I. Reading Physics

II. Human Theory

III. Fusion

This book is dedicated to my best friend, Suzanne Brodie.

When people ask her how she knows such fabulous and interesting things, she responds, "Because I live in the world."

I. Reading Physics

Gecko and Firefly

for David Sosnowski

Somewhere a hit man is feeding his pet gecko
live fireflies in the dark and noticing their deaths

only when the light doesn't blink back on. This
is how God works, you think, everyone a

firefly for some chameleon throat. The gecko
merely an organism like a car accident, leukemia.

Sometimes you're the pet gecko and you consume
other lives. Maybe if you were a gecko suddenly

and someone's pet, not even a god's, fireflies could
taste like chocolate, Godivas or like Tiramisu

or steak. And you'd be grateful. But what if you
were a vegetarian gecko? Maybe you'd stop eating

the winking beetles, falling in love with their light
not light, like the pulse of a star. And this god,

why is he feeding the gecko these tinkerbells?
Somewhere, almost anything is happening.

There might be a gecko god who eats other gods
and feeds people to fireflies who don't eat them

but shine their way like intermittent haloes.
But that hitman we've left alone with the night

Has one friend and it's the gecko. If we set
the gecko free, of what will that god not

be capable? as he sees the fireflies, like a net
of capture, wielding their flashlights across the field.

Reading Physics

for Shuko Wada Myer, artist

It's like a secret code you knew
as a child when you kept careful

notes of how exactly red ball gum
differs from blue when its shards shear off

in arcs floating in the space of hot tap water,
green plastic coffee cups laid out on your

yellow kitchen table in rows labeled like
petri dishes. Or like the red-yellow-blue

Play-Doh you melted on General Electric
bulbs in the dining room, dripping to candle

taper perfection, kept in Mason jars like
radium. Now, how steady state theory

seems to connect to the Maya beliefs - *We*
are now in our fifth world—and finite parts

of quantum suggest Egyptian star religion.
But also because there's something in chaos

theory akin to how you orbit your own world
unsent thank you notes spilling out of a desk

like filaments of novas, faulty wiring in the
basement contributing to certain eclipses upstairs.

Attraction and gravity not far from that Laurence
Olivier look-alike at the gym, extra laps around

the solar system for you, elliptical anomaly and
spiral galaxies happen every day in your coffee cup

when the cream swirls like so many billion
your Milky Way red as a spectrograph with foam

a sprinkle of cinnamon can make. Your eyes are not
the singularity expected with their darker nucleus and

so, fractal decisions become small town talk
of the nebular. You've left your one dimension for ten,

interlocking as Lincoln Logs your cousin
wouldn't let you play with and every time Hubble

makes a discovery no one can fathom, you applaud
like the fan of an underdog playoff team. It's great

to know minds who know calculus are stumped.
And you read and read far into the candlelit night

while mortality groans on its axis, as if, looked at
another way, your life has a solution some other

continuum could tell you.

Tomatoes

Like a cat, I lick the salt from
sliced tomatoes on a dish white

as goat's milk and think of you who grew
them in your back yard, the very vines

of Burton suburbia. You were so sure then
that everyone in the world liked fresh tomatoes

you wanted to give them free to the homeless
seeds yellow as 19th century wedding bands.

The love apple, red billows of a poisonous
ball gown the Puritans would not take into

their mouths as if they knew each had its own
sex secret, that red aorta undulating its way

between classifications of berry, fruit,
vegetable, no respect for botanical caste

taking all and none, so like you. I was
thinking how you loved each one of them

like a vice, salt and peppered into juice
or cooked whole into murderous pulp

in your spaghetti sauces, how after that wife
that house were gone, you dreamed linguini

and basil for those fleshy magenta lips, all
your sadness skinned and stewed whole

how you bred them still, tended like harem
daughters, something to do with women

how, back then, they must have tasted
light years away when you were so unhappy

gleaming like red dwarf stars
in the cellar of heaven.

Double Existence

"The event horizon is where, probably alternate universes exist." —Empires of Time

In some parallel universe
my mother is an opera star
satellite of the velvet world
the perfect diva of her age.
Successful from the first tour
raves and recording contracts
imprint like ducklings. She never
cans 48 quarts of tomatoes in a single
Saturday, divorces an alcoholic husband.

All because this time
when her high school teacher
asks to adopt her to Europe
for extended voice training
she pleads with disquieting piety
vows to make the parents rich.
When they say yes, they feel
her luminary gravity pull away.

She still likes rhubarb pie but adds
rich sauces of Paris to her repertoire
becoming heavier, never reads
the *National Geographic*. Instead,
gives interviews, sighing over her lack
of children. She retires to Belgium
not Houghton Lake, Michigan, keeps
her hair long and because she chooses
singing, without the double packs
of L&Ms every day for forty years
is still alive.

Eating a Star

The first point breaks in half,
drops easily into my maw. The esophagus
does its work as willingly as the molars.

It tastes crunchy with a bit of salt
The surprise is how easy to consume one.
There are no repercussions.

No gas clouds forming. No explosions
redistributing hydrogen or compactions
so dense, light bends. No. But then,

I am in a Burger King, Lake Forest,
Illinois where even the King has
shuttered his orange neon sign in favor

of the neighborhood style rules.
You'd almost miss this one with its
chestnut shingles.

But the star is quite gone now
a bit of whimsy that they've sizzled
up for kids and I realize

those other gold zigzags were
supposed to be lightning
bolts.

I don't know why the King tries
so hard. Hardly anyone notices
and minutes drone on like bees.

As the afternoon swirls around me
this sunshine is made even
sunnier because someone

is squeegieing the windows
(which are already clean) for
an elevated wage, since

this is the Lake Forest of *Gatsby*
where Tom Buchanan got his
string of polo ponies. I can only

be in that galaxy America
where I'm eating stars and lightning
bolts and thinking how homesick

I am for reality, like how everyone here
wears only ecru and white. I've
never seen such pristine tennis shoes.

It's a scary July. None of the kids whine!
The little pods are full of ennui at
five. So, I guess eating stars,

to them, or even lightning
bolts is just business.
The business of Kings reigns here.

But tonight, when the medflies
mount the whirlpool of light before
the parking lot lamps, I'll be glad

not to be a teenager here, where
the stars of the drive-thru
wait to snap like bolts

of envy out of the blue.

Dark Matter

Physics term, page 143, The Life of the Cosmos

My sister could not see
this step-father already
had a daughter.

Invisible dark matter
is the answer

He could not see that
his daughter, Connie, ellipsed
further and further away.

to missing mass, mass
that should be there

Her love like an elliptical orbit
something that should be there
mathematically, emotional biology.

but is not perceived
readily as hidden planets.

We cannot see past
some things. Mary hugged
him in the hospital

There is not enough light
to illuminate gravity

and still he stiffened. Less
visits came from Connie.
He died without

planetary observations
are linked to intelligent life

ever seeing her face looking down
as my sister's had.

on other galaxies and
if we cannot perceive them

When she planted
the rosebush on his grave
and it began to rain

it begins to look bad
for the existence of sentient life

she kept digging into
that dark matter as if
there was an answer

in any form, carbon-based
or silicon or something else

the rosebush almost tipping
out of her hands
like the tilting

how dark matter drifts
almost asleep behind things

of a natural law
no love coming up from that
ground ever.

yet how it is the answer
to heavy mass

The blackness of the loam
equaled the inheritance
she eventually received

and now we think a new way
about elements that should be there.

not Connie. And we could see
this balance clearly
and other dark matters.

Magic Realism

In Haiti they dream of snow
so blindingly believable
that flakes become etched in their irises
hexagons blink mirages
of sleet, dunes of snow.
Summer is a blizzard of white fever
Each step a snowshoe print
on the planet's slow turn.
They tell their voodoo:
Take the ice from us.

Here, Midwest snow
is common as pie dough.
You could live on it like manna.
Our four season sustinence
is a wheel
that moves like instinct
deliberate as a tractor.
When our heart's winter
moves against us
we know what to do.
Build snowmen. Lie down as angels.
No matter what the Celsius
we know summer
will take the ice from us.
It is our voodoo
our rage and sleep.

Black Holes

for Stephen W. Hawking

The essential metaphor of the universe is birth.
Think of it, the way the event horizon crowns
at the outside and will not let any pain escape
as how no light can run from its sectional borders.

On its other side, a new universe blooms
Though this is, as yet, unproven as reincarnation.
So, death swirls stars behind and there is no more?
Doubtful, given the nature of energy and matter.

At least on that side, there is a darkening push that
blacks you out, your consciousness gone as missing
mass or those planets of other galaxies unseen for
centuries. While inside ticks a brain of time.

The next future and the next is calculated when
stars or people collapse. My mother's private
universe ends when mine begins. So black
holes cost everything and nothing, the way

a heart fibrillates and restarts during birth, its
hardest muscle strains the star to maintain
itself. And the placenta whooshes like its
own galaxy let out from some eternal pulse.

The regeneration is what's untrustworthy.
That there was anything before me I cannot fathom.
Will my stars whiten to dust? Will there
be any more dreams like the Milky Way?

THE NUMBER OF APPLES

must explain the first snow apple
you ever saw, unsprayed
not grocery store boxed
the round in square holes.
And the sad ones, hanging on
or who had fallen
not to bushels and baker's palms
but to earth
tiny whorls in the back orchard
where you'd never seen anything
so pale and pockmarked.
The tender worm holes
like brown haloes
the soft spot on your baby sister's head
like the vaccination orb
on your older sister's arm
before you knew the words:
virus, decay.

And besides the gaudy Golden Delicious
upright Jonathan Smith
and the myths
the number of apples
is here to explain
these bruised ones
embracing all of its fruit
loving the very strangeness like a curator
holding onto the stems
of these gnarled, unharvested ones
suspended and celestial
like undiscovered planets
that have nothing do to
with earth or worms.

Satellite Father

for my older sister, Marilyn

When she was no longer eleven, in her party
dress of pink gingham and bows,
her father took her out like a debutante

for a spin and slowed the rusted Dodge
in front of a tavern, whose green neon
script said *Old Grandad* and *Malt Liquor.*

"I'm going to meet some people," he said,
"You stay here," a secret like a new cocktail
her head nodding below the half rolled down

window with its leaden chrome banding it
like the circlet on his cigar as he unwrapped
that quick as any present, headed away from her.

From the car seat she could play
with the mylar knobs on the radio
that didn't quite receive a station, kick

the plastic seat bottom sticking to the backs
of her legs like fly paper near their kitchen table.
Her patent leather heels tiny black pendulums

in 4/4 time, just missing each other, a rhythm
like the blues, lifting the backs of her small calves
off like bandaids, hugely slow at first, then faster

tempo, then tired kicking for nothing else to do
as 11:30, 12:15, 1:10, finally 2:15 whispers from
the luminescent green dial of the car clock

like the green cheese of the moon somewhere
outside, your father somewhere outside, the dark
of the car's black space, the only face she sees

until he staggers elliptically toward the Dodge
the orbit of one wingtip around the gravity
of cement curbs, pulling it down gingerly as

Neil Armstrong would later in her own
lifetime, that step for others, that non step bounce.
If it had been me in that six cylinder vehicle

swinging short legs, pounding the upholstery
with the fists of my heels, not knowing what
to do about him, saddening like the droop of pink

rose petals picked too early, in the echo of that
darkening street, all my thoughts loud as comets.
If it had been me, reeling on the ride back

crisscrossing the center lines of streets like
equators, I couldn't have looked up at him
as if he were the first full moon in history

no tread of humans on his face. And I,
a stage of the earth, at which nothing much
had yet begun to happen.

SCORING THE TEST

After a red giant dies, could gases alone form a new sun?
—Michigan Education Assessment Program test question.

I fill in the circle point.
Graphite shaving its head for me
and the boy who wrote:

A comet could pass through
the gas cloud, thereby
creating a new star. Where'd

he get *thereby* at Coleman,
a small school near Flint?
His playmates don't exhibit

his what if? or word play.
He gets a zero, same as they do.
No creative points.

Another writes: *If god wanted*
there to be a star, he could
just say it and there would be

a star even out of gases.
She hails from Christian Academy
recalling, maybe Adam rising

"even" out of dust. She goes on
with jump rope authority citing
labyrinths and nebulae

birthplace of stars. No points either.
I look around at fellow scorers
teachers cordoned in rows,

their lime and orange sweaters
out of shape as they are.
Heads bent like wild nodding

onion plants. No wildness here.
The room a cinderblock story problem
and only one answer.

A brief *No, needs*
dust and fusion
coldly wins full points.

But there's no galloping speculation
as in *Who is there when stars*
are formed? Are you? scratches

out a wiser, varsity Newton
on the brink of philosophy.
A teenage biologist pens

A star is not a plant.
And who can argue?
The question

is wrongly phrased.
We all know it. The cursive
they have missed the point

how red giants and white dwarfs
inhabit the vacuum space of dreams.
My leaden dot dilates like a pupil

looking into dark matter.
Event horizons shudder
with desire, hot, dense light.

Children *want* there to be stars
kajillions of them, never running
out like a summer hose forever spilling

infinity ON in the nuclear heat.
If you threaten their existence,
stars and minds will invent

a better physics
where wider theorems
and gymnastic formulas make it so.

You Are A Galaxy

Based on the elements of Drake's Equation
N= N(8) x fs x fp x fr x fl x fi x ft x L
which calculates the likelihood of contact
with another sentient life form in the universe.

You are a galaxy.
A small one, perhaps, spiraling out
of control at times, bumping into others
like bandsaw teeth at cross angles
but you have not yet imploded.

One day you decide to ride
the subway with new people.
Get off one stop early.

Perhaps you are in a fog
the shape of a horse head or crab
or millions of years in a day when
you are feeling elliptical.

There are new suits reading
the same *New York Times*
only two homeless
at this hour, fresher somehow.

But you are a galaxy.
You have been around as long
as your birth—what felt like
billions of centuries to your mother
and out came you
spinning, full of gas
and energy.

The metro spins you through
its dark chute and you think of your
subway crony, even the tall
woman who never looks at you.

Next, take those thoughts
whirling around you like planets:

When will I die? Why can't I avoid it?
Who will love me? What is safe?

She is unaware of your adventure.
You think how drab yesterday was
how each time you looked across
from your office

When will your environment
be stable? Growing thoughts
outward as crystals.

into the glossed windows of the edifice
you're now investigating like
a gumshoe in *True Detective.*

Then, how long before a civilization rises
up in you? Are you isolated as
Mir?

No one knows where you are
not your wife, asleep and dreaming
landlord or boss.

And, also, how will you discover
the thoughts of other galaxies,
the shadows of your suns' rays
blinding you to them?

Who are those people
who always look happy to you
in chrome silks, robust tweeds?

And your fires faint radio signals
random events, perceived as missing
mass, the "extra" background light.

"Bye," you say to the woman
with too many bags, soiled Nikes
thinking only of that tower

Then, how long before prime
numbers? How long before
$E=mc^2$?

awaiting retirement, the numbers
clicking by, that tower called
to you like Rapunzel.

How long before the first shaky
lightspeed
"Hello"?

It called like every siren
every dream. You its firefighter
and its dreamer.

This is the essence of Drake's equation
possibility of intersection across space.

And now you're traveling there
like an ambassador or Ponce de
Leon, your heart twinkling.

But there is one other element
added to the mix.

The tower's plaque says 1945
and a young girl with a camera
is looking at it, too.

All day later you're happy just
remembering this encounter,
the woman whose grandfather crashed

in which all other factors may come
together like the right poker hand
a full house.

into the tower before it was named
Trump, a World War II pilot in the fog

Yet, the worry of a royal flush
comes, long robes sit across
from you, cards close
to his chest of nuclear power.

 and how you've come out of
 your own fog today, triumphant

The dice is marked on all
sides: religion, politics.

 that you've made contact
 and look forward to events coming
 toward your own horizon:

One die is loaded

 What will happen next, what you
 can still know about your possible selves
 no longer burnt out as dead suns

so that another galaxy is, at the same time,
roiling your way.

 not finished as veneer
 but ready

You are a galaxy
in which the number of contact
is either as large as pulse time or small as a fractal moment

 even glad for that downed navigator
 his granddaughter coming as you did

either infinite or finite matter.

 to finally see the other side of something.

You are a galaxy.
 You are the Milky Way.
 Two people 23 billion light years away.

II. Human Theory

Effects of Alcohol

Plants don't get drunk.
That's because plants don't drink alcohol.
But if you wanted to get a plant drunk,
say, a pine tree or a begonia
and you poured the Jack Daniels
into the soil and the plant drank
up the whiskey through its roots
it still wouldn't get drunk
because the alcohol
like acid on briancells,
disintegrates the roots
and the plant dies. Death being
the only known cure for a hangover.

Maybe the plant decides ahead of time
to chuck the headache and nausea.
Maybe plants get wretched hangovers
and death is preferable to torture.
Or maybe Nature decides she doesn't want
any drunks in the meadow.
You can't have saplings staggering in at dawn
Redwoods knocking over picnic tables.
Like the plants, humans, too, know the cure.
It just takes them a little
longer to get there.

Divination

In the middle ages, it was believed that true dowsers
could find more than aquifers and springs.
Superstitions of the Middle Ages, 1934

Can't you do it sometimes?
When a lone hawk circles above you
on your walk to the grocery, gliding,

almost talking to you, the way it hovers
each feather a syllable. Next day:
a letter arrives, a stranger is coming.

As if those talons carried broadcast news
in their yellow grip. Calm floats down
like one gray feather scissoring air.

Or say you're on a train and can feel
more than the locomotive, the pull of time,
years of a choice yearning into you.

That night, you meet someone who's trouble.
Later, you recall that tug in the time
line, him pulling you like the pull

of steel wheels across rails. Not like
when a phone rings, that cordless umbilical.
You guess it's a friend who promised

to call sometime. This isn't it.
One day, driving by a road, you look
down its white, painted stones

know you'll be there soon. That
road's taken but unchosen. You get
lost, find a doorbell that rings

a strong man in a blue shirt. Then
you marry or move but the point
is that early warning, unexpected,

secret compartment in the briefcase,
yellow dog by the side of the road.
These are all I've seen come true. Not like

a newspaper horoscope but like a sure
photograph, daguerreotype, steel engraving.
It rises inside you like a storm coming

over the prairie for hours and hours
building to a lightning strike that takes
down the whole red barn. This white

filament of burst ozone is true—
and you douse your way over
a known landscape

led but also leading
your creased palms
to water or murder or gold.

FATHER GHOST

What I remember of you is not a voice
or father's light hand on his daughter
but the Milky Way candy bar you gave me
once, after being gone a long time.
When you disappeared again, smell of your cigar
hung in the air like ectoplasm.

The ghost of that visit seems hazy now
though you were the most real thing
I knew then—your outline the clearest
if only an outline. Like chalk marks
discover the day after—
proof spirits moved furniture.

Your details haunt me now, the dates
I can't resolve. How can you be my
Father with your 1897 birth date
in an entire other century?

I carry your hair and eyes, tendency
toward liquor, name, and this milky
way of reaching toward a universe
where we might talk and listen.

Water Witching

Our crops have blistered open, our own
skin and eyes split by roaring sun.
You say sea water has the exact
composition of human blood.
We believe you more than ever.
What else can we do?
We have no power.

You wield the branch of our life
or death: a triangle
cornerstone of pyramids
symbol of impossible magic
as water seems to us now.
Your hands, lined like parched riverbeds
from years of directing hope
intersect the dusky horizon.
Heat surrounds u though it is almost night.

Like a heartbeat, water pumps below
and you, a doctor with stethoscope extended
stop at the sound of health.
Your arms shake like twigs in a thunderstorm.
It could almost rain.
You stop shaking
drop tool to dry loam and say:
"Dig here."

We pay you with many coins, rejoicing.
Our shovels glint in the dark.
Each time we tire in the heat
you say, "Deeper."
You know that humans and water
are the same everywhere.
Thirst is just a matter
of how far down you're willing to go.

Nth

"Nth designates the last numerical event in a series."

Here are the things I know for certain:
Your father named you after a minor sci-fi movie

Monster and when your mom, my sister, discovered
this, she was mad. But he had the spelling wrong

and it came out like a feudal English lord, so that
was all right. And one time on the swing set, you

screamed out: "Ma, Su and Ray, Sue and Ray!"
because you could see your playmates' parents

haul in from the two-tone Chevy and were excited
as fizzies. This was when you were only

seven, so we made fun of your intensity
tried to blare our sea horse chords like

your bullfrog lungs in imitation, but you
smiled, shiny as chrome on that hard, high swing.

Once, when Marilyn, your other aunt, wanted you
to clean your plate, she made up a song, "Potato chips,

potato chips, crunch, crunch, crunch! Come on, Cory,
eat your lunch!" When you got into trouble with her

later, she said, "Man, you can beat that kid but he just
won't cry." I knew it was bad, somehow. And your

older brother, Guy, fell for Marilyn's trick of letting
you stay behind (when you whined you didn't want

to go to the park) but secretly she stole back to scare
you two as you stepped down the second floor

landing, hugging that spidery railing like
a drop-off buoy. Guy pushed you in front of him

when she sprang out like firecrackers from a least
likely place. He yelped, "Yah-ah-ahhhh!" with

the full terror of a ten year old. But you said nothing
as we laughed like baby monkeys. Later, tired

of your fighting, Marilyn got real boxing gloves
from her football husband, Ken, staged a three-round

bout and when you beat your older brother bloody,
two black eyes to your lone shiner, we cheered you

loud, louder, LOUDEST. And at seventeen
the second oldest of six, you moved out of your

father's house after some dispute, but wrote later
(all congenial) and your mother dreamed of you

playing a kind of dulcimer she'd never seen before
and you started up a business, married a gorgeous

southern woman, Ruth, had three kids an then,
in a van, late one night, used a shotgun like

your dad's whiskey chaser of Drewry's beer
and that was all.

ANTHROPOLOGY

Downstairs, in a house built at the turn of the century
is a scrapbook of photographs on heavy, glued paper
glue from horses too old to ride.

In one book at the bottom, almost trying to be missed
next to the posed black and whites of the Great Wall
and the Parthenon and some temple in Malyasia

and the skeleton assemblages in the Cappuccini Crypt
under a thirteenth century monastery is one photograph
of a fourteen-year-old girl, black hair, white teeth, olive

skin, perfectly formed and sensual breasts.
The breasts are unadorned and she has no jewelry and
her eyes are opaque as two ebony doors painted over

with lacquer. I can imagine the photographer's
glee and what he told her, or her mother, or father
about having to get a "sample" that this was science.

I am not that sophisticated. I don't care that he perhaps
paid her or her family and they ate well that day
and this is how things were done. There is anger.

I can tell because it throbs not like something erotic
because of her eyes. If the photographer did not
give away his soul, he is behind me now, begging

me to look at his artistry and I refuse. I leave him
in that sweaty moment in his ill-fitting waistcoat, boots
leathery as his brow became in that shutter of time.

I know he died unmarried or if married, unhappy, or
if happy, she left him. It is all the doom I am allowed
to fit in this square of words, my photograph

of the eye that wants document, lens irretrievable
as that moment when her not yet eyes, liquid,
yielded to this look, hard as obsidian. She is older

than a century, now, older than daguerreotype.
She is the oldest child I have ever seen.

Exotic

I am a topless dancer
at LLT's Showbar or Vasquo's.
I am blonde and twenty-two.
Venus de Milo with arms.
Lace and leather
for every occasion.
Whips, chains, stiletto heels.

I never show pictures
of my children
eyes lost as dimes
down city sewer grates
or tell the name
of my live-in boyfriend
his underworld biker pals.

I tell every suit
and blue collar
that I am doing
social research
for a Harvard thesis.
Even though they don't
believe me at first
I rattle off
statistical studies

like tickertape
on Black Tuesday.
I crash your dreams.

I reap life histories
like a John Deere thresher
at August harvest.

Blackmail is my life.

VAMPIRES AT THE LAUNDROMAT

All the women are thin, stick-like
in their leftover clothes, pale as white ash.
There are apparitions of plaids and stripes:
the wrong thing with the wrong thing.
A woman in a gold print skirt pulls
her raspberry top down over orange stockings
flashes fiery fingernails catching clothes
in supernatural shapes.
Men discuss what would be cheaper
in the long run: laundry or wives
holding cigars as the spin cycle
drones on like neon. The bats
in the dryers
are trying to stay upside down.
You don't dare put your hand in.

Here is the ritual of the unliving
the frozen ones, tired and helpless.
You are afraid of changing their rhythm.
The glass doors yawn open, say:
Get out while you can.
No one is in charge or talks
or notices dark skies outside where
a storm swells with threat, the lightning.
This is the Vampire Laundromat
open twenty-four hours a night
where washers rattle like skeletal bones
and the zombies stay with you
like the machines
and nothing gets clean.

Moving Furniture

I hated moving furniture.
The green couch refused to give up
its routine near the coffee table,
ruts beneath its feet deep as worry about money.
I could never remember exactly how we *did*
move it, sweating, resting a full ten minutes
after shoving the big lug, arms and back thick
as wrestlers we saw every Saturday on TV.

Nor was shifting the stuffed rocker into
a new corner easy, like moving a bachelor
out of his apartment. But every Spring
for no reason I could see, my mother moved
furniture, dusted, waxed, Pine Sol-ed,
Chloroxed, complained, wanting, I think now,
to change her life through the agency of sofas and lamps.
Like Sisyphus, she learned there are only so many
places a boulder or an end table can go.

I liked window cleaning best, the gleaming
sapphire Windex icy spray. It must be how a man
feels with the right tool for edging a lawn.
Armed with the *New! Improved!* nozzle
and twenty paper towels, I could make transparent
the world, as if everyone's seeing more clearly
depended on my ability to erase the streaks
of prism, redbluegold in the beveled glass.

The fluidity of its original firing revisited
in those glinting occlusions that bested me
every Spring on those two French doors
the blonde wood stiff as Marilyn's hair.
Those tiny boxes like cells in your skin ticking
or that one month you gave up smoking.
The clarity, even in 1967 when we held
our breath: Russian spies, Brown vs.
Board of Education, Nixon's speeches.

Meanwhile, sans revolution, my mother
was moving furniture. I was cleaning the lenses
of our house to see a better world, like a geisha,
as if arranging components
of living was enough to alter history.
It wouldn't stop my five years with a bad boyfriend,
giving up a child for adoption or my mother's
protracting lung cancer.

But these mornings *are* our history, made of
Windex and Chlorox in a rustbelt city
in the Midwest, last century. Every obstacle
in my life has been that green couch
that would not move, and especially the sun-streaked
rays of beveled French doors
currently opening for no one.

If Sin is a God

Sin is the name of one of the Babylonian gods in the Gilgamesh Epic.

If Sin is a god . . .
I might have found religion.

In fact, might already be an acolyte.
Maybe high priestess. Do I get

some kind of ring or scarlet robe?
Since most of Babylon has crumbled, there's

no big book to scrap about and learn.
Just twelve tablets in clay, simple verse.

Maybe it is removed by a millennium
or two but think how there's no hymns

to learn maybe just a motley bunch
of folks like myself or you. Really, aren't

your friends the ones who tell you things
you thought you didn't want to know

until you do? And this guy, Sin, can't be
all bad if there's such an awful lot of him still left

in every corner of the globe. Isn't it a comfort
someone watches someone everywhere?

Think of the rituals one might do.
But even if it's true there's no one left

to worship Sin as he was accustomed
in those far off, golden Uruk days

I'm sure he'd allow this member in good
standing in. You find faith where you can.

Letter From Jeptha's Daughter

Jephtha's Daughter
In the Book of Judges, Jephtha promises to sacrifice the first thing he sees on returning from a successful battle. His daughter is the first thing he sees to whom he gives a four year reprieve before fulfilling his obligation by killing her.

These four years have spilled
like salt from a shaker.
You know how it gets.
Wood needs shaping.

Or the fire goes out. The cold demands
more sewing. Or something always
must be washed, purified.
And I forget where I am

what day, how many left. I stare out
at mountains so like the rise
of your shoulders. Do you
think of me when you pray?

Do you pray it is a dream?
I know there is no—only . . . some days
are full of sun. Thrushes warble
such ballads of longing.

I think I am winged in the cedars.
Indigoes and purples rise along sunset mists.
At twilight, it looks as if I could step out
on a cloud solid as those gray stones

near our home. I imagine a bridge
where oaths spill like lentils into ashes
ashes spill into having the waiting over.
See you soon.

Template

Today I saw a man walk willed
into woods. His ex- and new wife,
son and life outside factories

trailed after, each facet a direction
of his flat universe. Each a corner
of his template.

I thought how like a stencil
the frame of his story's shape:
would it turn out five-pointed star

or the letter H? A man was born.
He lived and he died. The end.
Template for nineteenth century novels

and tombstones. What do you fill it with?
Our DNA template for Milky Way, maybe.
Fetal stages template for evolution.

Each tadpole can turn human, each human
turn pterodactyl. Our tails disappear
like fingers in mittened flippers of the blue whale.

Shape comes and goes by rule of templates.
But the man entering the woods does not let
circumstance bind him. He knows the model

of his life like the hood ornament on a Mercedes.
His new wife has no fins and will never be
a pterodactyl. His son is not entirely carnivore.
The man stays until midnight.

When he looks up, he puts
a template over stars.
Out walk: lions, bears, warriors, gods.

Divining Rod

Water, metal, treasure, murder. These four you find.

Aquifers older
than the first
thought of
Egypt, gold
in long lodes
booty and the
body of a
woman in
the barrel
strangled by
her husband.

Each is the same
to you
amoral as bark.

How is a
strangled woman
like a
bar of silver?
Cut from hazel,
mahogany, ash,
preferably singled
out by lightning:
messenger and
squealer.

How is a
murderer
like loot?
The guilty quake
ores shuffle from
comfortable
beds, streams
and the dead
confess each crime
of isolation.

In your wake: vengeance, greed, measure, thirst.

The Language of Flowers

At first, we had only a few clues: the whisper
of temptation form an apple blossom
the sadness brought with dead leaves.
But with care and study
whole phrases began to come out.
We listened. We took notes.

It's love at first sight! cried the coreopsis.
I will always be true! howled the azaleas.
You are cruel! cried a stinging nettle.
Once we had them talking, we couldn't listen enough
Activity! shouted the thyme.
Curiosity! a sycamore.

Long arrangements of petal and leaf
were concocted by shrewd botany linguists
It was the new science. It caught on.
Everyone sent letters of bloom to lovers
friends, even lenders in business.

As in all gardens, a problem arose:
misinterpretation.
If you received a scotch broom
did it compliment your neatness or humility?
Did it imply that neat people had humility?
The same foxglove blossom heard chanting
Sincerity, in the next instant could intone *insincerity.*
Suspicion grew like mushrooms.

We began to wonder how we had started.
There were long silences between lovers.
None could remember the sound of flowers.
Was it their vocal chords
or music heard in a dream?

We returned to our gardens
where the cloves were aloof.
If flowers had words
they were in photosynthesis

long conversations of perfume.
Their speech a deep mystery
even to themselves.

We grow the same.
Our precarious dialogue
in the matrix of our hearts.
Our language the language of flowers.

Inventions

for Gladys Randall Kearns
1920-1991

She always said
to think up clever
gadgets that would
make a lot of money.

Madam C. J. Walker, Millionaire
Innovative African American cosmetics
1867-1919

My library card
was an experiment
in scratched out signatures
and written-over late fines.

Bette Nesmith Graham
Inventor, White-out
1924-1980
Corporate holdings: 40 million
Mother, Mike Nesmith, The Monkees

No women inventors except
Marie Curie with her radium dreams.

Betty Galloway
patent for bubble making
machine, 1964, aged 10

Reading in the dark
of the hallway lamp
was my only experiment with light.

Improvements in pyrotechnic
night flare signals
Martha Coston
1826-1896

I wanted to solve her single-
parent muscle spasms, her dreams
of large, brick homes.

Computer innovator
Grace Hooper
Mother of COBOL
1908-1992
Rear Admiral, U.S. Navy

Her first notion
was a band worn
around the wrist
tight as a safe's dial.

First African American
banking institute
Annie Turnbo
1864-1912

The band was your personal
air conditioning system
transferring humidity with sweat.

Instruments to measure
specific gravity of liquids
Hypatia, mathematician, Greek
370-415 BCE

We had market
because everyone
wants to be cool
as a blue cucumber.

Development of indigo
as a commercial crop
Eliza Lucas Pickney
1722-1793

But this daughter never
dated boys who took shop,
had no electric wiring talents.

Stephanie L. Kwaleck
inventor, kevlar fiber
Uses: from bullet-proof
vests to space vehicles
born 1923; 28 patents

I didn't even have the plot
of how to make this
success story.

Widely regarded as inventor
of the first novel:
The Tale of Genji
Murasaki, Shikibu
978-1030, Japan

Her next idea involved
weather, an early warning
system for tornadoes.

Dr. Sara Josephine Baker
first American to institute
preventive medicine, New York
City tenements, 1873-1945

She read in *National Geographic*
how barometric pressure
predicts whirlwinds. I could never
have predicted what
happened next:

Inventor, Frankenstein
Mary Wollstonecraft Shelley
1750-1890

Back to the volumes of fact:
Our Weather World and *Meteorology:*
Past is Future

Reinvented age of hominids back
37 million years, Mary Leaky,

finder of "Nutcracker Man" skull,
first fossil footprints
born 1913

as if I could pound
together any box
of flashing warning.

Internal structure of crystals
Dorothy Crowfoot Hodgkin
born 1910
Nobel Prize Chemistry

Nimbus clouds and cirrus
were as mysterious to me
as her breed of orange strawberries
I learned later were a new hybrid.

Barbara McClintock
gene transposition in crops
1902-1992
Nobel Prize Genetics

The berries were smaller, more orangey.
They made a sound, falling,
quiet as breast lumps.

Ruth Handler
1928-1985
Inventor, Barbie, also
first flexible prosthetic
for mastectomy patients
Combined profits: 500 million

But she didn't write it up
or name the fruit *Gladys rosaceae fragaria.*
She grew them for her children
and people she liked.

Irene Joliet Curie
daughter, Marie Curie
enzyme discoveries

1897-1956
Nobel Prize Chemistry

Even though I learned a lot
about weather
like the walled cloud's
erratic spinning

Inventor, modern
dance of pure expression
Isadora Duncan
1878-1927

just as the spiral
balances
before destruction.

Fannie Farmer
Exact measurements
in cooking
1857-1915

One photograph showed
it hovering
big as a spaceship.

Rachel Carson
Environmental effects of DDT
Pulitzer Prize for Silent Spring
1907-1964

And I wondered if most
UFOs were really these clouds
dense as granite
hovering like my mother's thoughts.

Dr. Lise Meitner
Co-inventor, nuclear fission
Denied Nobel Prize
later reinstated on research team
1922-1965

III. Fusion

Barbed Wire

"In the 1880's, enough barbed wire was produced to reach the moon—and back."
—voiceover, Frontier House, *documentary, PBS*

Say it's true:
a pewter fish line spiked
with intermittent

hooks, a wire hanging
from the moon, its stud,
the earth a dangling earlobe.

Metal rope makes
a kind of sense. I can see
ranchers lassoing Artemis'

light, hanging the planet
from it like a painting of man.
Yes, the moon: a white nail

on which to arrange things.
Tilt the wall of the solar system
until it matches the drapes,

a bit of design work here:
the dulled, silver thorns
counting off miles. Tin stingers

digging in, sectioning night
like a plumb line and (who
was it?) said, *Give me an edge*

to lean against. My fulcrum
moves the world.

Termite Love

"You have given me wings of white ants." Ugandan saying meaning you've given me nothing. White ants = termites who have only 15 minutes to mate before their wings fall off and they die. —for Jerry Bleem, artist

Not as bad as it sounds
this lithe stratum of almond slivers
the oblong arcs of vein
The bodies of termites
must be efficient as
below soil irrigation

a sienna brown. Though weightless
resonance remains of flight's
heavy bond, certain currents
wings dropping off
in fifteen minutes
anyway.

in the horse latitudes galloping by.
Transparent white, ghostlike
yet a certain integrity, a span
What does it mean
to speed date
in the webbed world?

between two cultures:
insect and human;
oxygen and cellophane.
Are instincts off
if your antennae
wobbles like a broken baton?

What still hovers
circles and spins like Sally Rand,
finds the right temperature and mates
Do you
miss
your station

in fifteen minute millenniums
before twin onionskins molt
like bark from white bamboo.

Will you flick your
moment away
like a cigarette

It's the bodies they eat in Uganda
a tasty, nutrient, crunch.
But wings give sustenance

or like fireflies losing their spark?
Cut short like
telephone conversations

only in the mind
as we think of them scattered
diaspora of crinoline

a hymen or fidelity
while others
wink a generation alive

one truckload weighing only
a gram of kozo, denying
their best part.

the Origin of Species
of one night
stands

I've never thought
about termites in love
their ethereal wings

sister of glass
sire of mica

but it must be
like us: a whirling of light
falling stars kissing

elaborated
thinness beyond
dimension

when knees radium
collarbones nova
what falls off us—not wings, exactly—
until nothing remains
but frothy
night.

and we swarm
and soar
past aurora borealis
to greater heights.

The Behavior of Spiders

"Omens were drawn from the behavior of spiders."
The Tale of Genji, *footnote, p. 35*
by Mirasaki Shikibu, The Imperial Court, Japan, 1010 AD

I.

Could a tree still be standing
where Mirasaki once stood?
Like this locust here, waving its feathered

greenery through only two centuries,
that I could touch and be one degree
from a writer who seems to me like Dorothy

Parker. Modern. Even removed by
millennium and literature that's lost
like The Haunted Journey, excised

forever since the fifth century. Mirasaki
herself, excised. She speaks not only
of love but intrigue fresh as still-vined

strawberries, orange and biting.
I see translation formality creeping
over her strong

conviction of the moment
like kudzu, a vine she knew
but by another name.

II.

What's lost, too, are the messages
of black widow, death's head, dappled
brown arachnids and their clairvoyance.

Not from biology but myth. What
omen does the half-finished web bring?
Do wind-blown strands mean death?

If no dew attaches, will the new
bride bear no children? Or are
tears the new diamonds?

She wouldn't be half as beautiful
if some of her wasn't lost
as I am in these pages and other

places I keep returning.
Through the corridors of paragraphs
I find pathways I might

have sauntered down,
aisles not completely
closed to me in either life.

III.

If not, if no bamboo or ginseng is standing,
still, no pillow book has brought another world
so completely formed—

a robin's egg, blue with life—and I can
see her here, swinging and sighing
in a hammock, her red and green

silk kimono, chest heaving at a twilight
sparrow, taking meaning perfectly
like blue thread upon the snow.

Secret Doors

I am always opening the secret doors of buildings
the neglected, painted over portals
        the ones they do not want you to see behind

the door frame part of the rococo wallpaper
the keyhole disguised as a plug—
        even oaken doors, numbers lightly embossed

out of order, unsupervised, opening to utilities
telephone intestines, part of nothing plumb, straight
        or true. Some impulse of design moves me.

I am always rewarded by the slatted, wobbly listing of
the souls of buildings, all Hitchcock camera angles
        the real thing next to the not real thing

discovering the chipped, 1920 terra cotta brick, the paint
splattered work paints, and once, a battered Playboy
        lunch bucket with "Gus" engraved on the side.

I want to see the guts in these grand excavations
lighting often a bulb and exposed wire, especially
        institutions of learning, especially

higher learning, all the molding and veneer.
Perhaps it is because no father ever showed me
        the wonder of lumber or five eighths fittings

and the songs of tools and carpentry were as foreign
as my mother's instructions of gloves and stillness
        as the mumblings of my father's hangover sleep.

Even so I am rarely embarrassed, unsure of my place, caught
by someone saying, "Hey, elevator's that way" or "Miss
        restroom's down the hall."

voice trailing off like the blinking light of the insane's
paddy wagon they imagine whirling me away like their
        own ditzy Aunt Shirley.

Peeking and prodding, I am just one more crazy woman
they add to the list, shaking their heads like the palm
of a child playing Parchesi. The dice in her hand

leading me to my next move like that woman in the wall
who lived in secret for four years, hidden in the house
of her childhood like a knickknack.

That woman, hair firecrackers, eyes dimmed
was high priestess to my religion, she said, "It was always
my home," as they led her away.

All her friends and family behind pine doors, behind
the granite and marble doors of mausoleums, behind all
that loss she survived, opening her first days.

She reminds me of Cicero, his famous dream, demanding
an infinite universe. He said, even if you got
to the end, what was on the other side?

Because he could imagine the other side of a door
he knew the universe was endless. Think of him thinking
always what was on the other side.

There will always be doors unopened, sealed by rainwater,
primered into background, neglected as assembly instructions
the shy child in the family of achievers.

Hidden as unlisted telephone numbers, the fossil
In the Mesozoic wave. These are the ones passed over
as Britons in blitzkrieg air raids

as the angel of death over certain families in Egypt
as a woman in a wall. And if locked, I am getting better
at jiggling the handle just so—

Loss Universe

(three voices)

Under the moon of the streetlight
the city child is winking out
like an early star.

One day you start to lose things:
telephone number, pocket knife.
No problem, you think.
The number is written down elsewhere.
You'll buy another Swiss Army.

Everything has to be somewhere
and it is: Good advice, ark of the covenant, car keys.

Running behind
this row of redberry bushes
or that stand of scrub pine

But then you lose the address book
in which the number slept
in the upstairs bedroom
of a blue-lined page marked K.

There is no map anymore to Loss Universe.
Flat atlas of limbo, blue veined avenues
circulatory system of gone cities

small as a pearl
in this sea of dark clams.

Things catch, fall out of pockets:
screwdrivers, scissors, slide toward oblivion
with I.D.s, codes, credit.

was burned: a gift to flame
like all the leaves of all the falls
you were lonely

This is the path
of the neighborhood child
who flees degenerate
or swaying dragon's shadow

You lose your mother's middle name.
Friends stop dropping by.

gone as 17 centuries of hieroglyphs
in a flash of ceremony.

Between the clapboard houses rows

You've lost them to some other highway

If you want something
to live forever
burn it.

The one place curved black fence wire allows
soft, thoughtless flesh through

while Kansas loses topsoil
the cities, patience
the whole Atlantic Ocean
its innocence

They are talking about this place.
Fire is the pretty sure door
to loss universe.

like a kind of northern light.

A whole book of sleeping numbers
empties from your life.

Do you remember saying
I'm not that person anymore?
They're here

In neighborhoods like these, I get lost

Your sense of humor is next
then regret.

They come with those
you loved
best and worst and first

I follow gravel tamped down
grass bent oddly.

Your life flies up from you
thin tape measure spiralling out

and you still loving
them on the wide
emotional trapeze

A late detective I look for markers
where youth has been.

like a yellow sunbeam waving good bye.

Here is everyone's
virginity:
how you felt before.

I want to verify these urban catacombs
and know myself

This is where the saying
you can't get there
from here originated.

their getaway.

Love and Plutonium

A student writes *plutonic love* instead of platonic.
But he is right, anyway.

Only nineteen, he has discovered
the truth: love is radioactive.
One face—a thousand ships launch.
One launch—a thousand cities vanish.

Love and plutonium
cause things to mutate:
mice becoming albino as clouds
or the heart sprouting wings.

Either atomic can be a bomb
or heat a home through winter.

Once born, neither love nor plutonium
can ever be got rid of,
not even buried in lead barrels
beneath a landfill
below a water table
behind a hello.

My student is so brilliant.

At ground zero, love *will* blow you up—
signaling a magnetic signature
long after its researchers
are alive.

Love and plutonium both glow in the dark.

The Planets Line Up

"Much speculation surrounds the lining up of all nine planets."
New York Times *article*

The occultist and the *New York Times* coffee man
read it over breakfast:
you are safest on high ground.
Watch for earthquakes, signs in the air.
Everything will be mutant and magic
disaster, a beginning.

This is how we celebrate
a lot of people stuck in miracles.
We wanted prophecy and the refuge to watch it.
What everyone said was larger than the moment.

Whoever had a telescope or eyes knew
the high pitch of Mercury, heard Earth's
sad drone clicking into place like special beads
Galileo's marbles discovering order.

Wherever technology was, it wasn't far enough:
Voyager, somewhere sleeping in the distance.
The moon spread its silver weight
like opium on the diaphragm
lifting us higher than fear.

The Last Twelve Minutes of the Magnificent Ambersons

what Ron said he wanted

Wouldn't you know he'd want something lost?
An ending spurned by producers who
wanted it happy, thwarting Orson Welles

lost as my mother's singing
larynx flat as a guitar pick
both still out there, echoing, according

to Science. Sound waves leap off the planet
like kids smashing through the Van Allen Belt
in a game of Red Rover.

Hop to moon. Skip to Mars. Each sun a yellow jump
rope. Solar systems like backyards, notes
bounding around a black hole, or

knowing my mother, causing one. Dark as the Dawson
Find, cache of silver nitrate souls
lost filmic ark found in the seventies

buried in Alaska, tossed to avoid shipping charges.
Pewter disks the only copies of Chaplin,
why we know him now.

Hope or physics saves these canisters, Welles' work
and my mother's intonation.
Her mezzo soprano cannot

be buried like those last twelve minutes
where Agnes Moorehead as Fanny
silently rocks as Eugene

leaves her forever. Forever in film is a long time:
the first time you see it
the twenty-second

re-encrypts longing. Forever in death
is a long time
like how music is.

Joseph Cotton's oaken timbre
recorded decades ago
or my mother

rocking and rocking good-bye
with her song like Welles'
deep focus.

Two figures, clearly seen
keep both stories together
one foreground, the other back.

This is why people
ask for the lost:
their story tiny, the world large.

And if my mother's voice is still ringing
in asteroids, then there *are* twelve minutes;
in some dark vault, uniting Ron

with his ending, my mother with me,
an aria over decades of blackness,
her voice nitrate, resilient as silver

that can be brought back up
out of earth, that can be mined
into the hammered light.

!!!!

Hark! Hark! Without us there are no headlines!
No *Lucky Strike Goes to War!* No *Dewey Wins!*

No *Earthquake Kills Thousands in China!*
No *WAR!!!* No *Life On Mars!*

Hark! Hark! How would you ever know
you're alive without us!! This is the succinct

underlining! This is the invention of the age!
We make it possible for the feeble to express

themselves! For youth to have a voice! For
the angry to tell someone off without expletives!

We are the surprise at the bottom of the rope!
We are a marching band! We are 10,000 bayonets!

We are a line of straight black cannons that go
Blam! Blam! Blam! Blam! at the absolute end!

???

Are you the embodiment of the meaning of life?
Who invented you? Was it some French scholar

tired of giving answers? Why are you shaped
like a black squid, squirting ink onto an unforgiving

page? How many ways could you be drawn without
being accusatory? How many of you does it take

to answer death? How many times have you wanted
to declaim? Do you like it when you dance with

exclamations? Does it make you feel schizophrenic?
Is everyone jealous of your mysterious nature?

Why are you sometimes shaped like a hook? Why
is it children do that when drawing you? When will

you take responsibility? And why is there
the point you make anyway, at the bottom, like

the tassel on a fez? Why are you sometimes like
the snail of a dark-haired girl's ponytail? Why

are you coiled to strike like the snake in the garden?
Why is it that in diaries of the oppressed your song

is *Why? Why? Why? Why? Why? Why? Why?*
Why are you the craziest? What gives you the right?

SEMI-COLON

Richard Hugo said you were ugly and when in doubt
not to use you; but no one can help wanting to feel

sophisticated sometimes; in fact, the sophistication
of semi-colons is something that comes with practice;

especially in Freudian psychology; it is when
one writes about the id, ego and super ego; that is,

there are other ways to use the semi-colon; for example,
explanations in a list as in the ego, the doer, the getter

of things; the id, the desirer, the *I want* of all things; the super
ego, the moral nay-sayer to all things; each of these is

imperative to bear in mind when using the semi-colon;
actually, the semi-colon was invented in 9000 b.c. Alexandria;

that the inventor was a librarian is no surprise; this date lives in
infamy in the minds of students; in fact, these minds despise the
rules of semi-colon;

they have no time to ponder with their busy lives;
these lives include ignoring semi-colons;

or they use semi-colons,
but always in incorrect ways that connect unrelated things;

of course, they occasionally use the semi-colon
correctly; thus, the lonely, misunderstood

semi-colon is ignored by writers; the sentences only
half formed or deformed; thus, the semi-colon is, as Hugo pointed

out, ugly indeed; ergo, it is another invention whose
purpose is forever obscured; that is the fate of the semi-colon.

Apostrophe

Your hand in the air like a will o' the wisp.
Your hand waving from Queen Victoria's carriage.

Your tail like a puppy's eager for the ball in the air.
Your hand like a comet's tail, trailing between

phrases that want to be together like estranged
lovers. You make fun of hoighty toighty things

by saying hamburger o' ketchup and tub o'
lard. You seem to want to connect all

things that are broken like the peacemaker
in a dysfunctional family. But you have other uses.

Why'n't we take the contractions, and roll them out?
You stand like zero, the placeholder for letters

gone AWOL. This plan can't work for long.
Sometimes letters are gone forever

like God's hooks = gadzooks and can never go back
to the brimstone scariness of hooks connected to

omnipotence and God's wounds = zounds! which
never again has the sadness translated into shock

just silliness. Without you, the world's in reverse
and people talk slower which isn't always a good thing.

You are concerned with what's whose. Sometimes as
possessive as a lawyer's alimony check. Mary's car

and the nucleus's dark center, Huntington's Chorea
for example, and John's condoms and Murphy's Law.

Territorial, but responsible for *It's gonna be okay* and
what about the glorious shan't in *Wuthering Heights*?

Plus rehabilitating ain't into *Webster's Dictionary*, plus
elided letters that equal a policy: should've could've would've.

Comma

Because of you, we go on indefinitely, sideswipe
death, run sentences like a treadmill, extend clauses

in the life contract, as if everything were
connected. You look like a sideways

eye of Horus, seeing all those things we add
to a list, our sentences shopping for meaning

without you, we would be more succinct
but, no, there's you, your leather jacket, the bad element

in a gang, urging us on, *go a little further, keep*
it up, don't turn back now, you can do it, that's

what you say, always get us in trouble
looking innocent as a galaxy

spiral arm on a further edge, feather boa
ice crystals, snow ghosts, whirling eyes

the grinding wheel, the Fates, see how easy
it is with you, like a karaoke band, like a safari

caravan, like a race car off its track, like a train
down the Alps, like an idotarod sledder, like an

emeritus professor, like the Sahara desert, like
immortality, like a lover, go on and on and on.

Cold Blue

It was that winter my sister and I
made the igloo you could die in
if snowplows worked their teeth just right.

The snow hadn't been stained yet
with the exhaust of cars, like how
the moon hadn't been walked on yet

no icicle flag pinning it like a collector's bug.
I fluffed down in drifts so deep I couldn't
breathe. The snow had a too-white color, leached

out, the blue of detergent or that new popsicle
coveted by grade schoolers in 1962 as cool,
something unproveable as blue-veined flesh

caught in Yukon frostbite, blue gills under
icy stream. We had heard but doubted that toes
break off like ice cubes in our frosted metal

trays, that fish eyes harden to coal. I didn't
understand then, the words: *uncertain, sure.*
I thought maybe this was what blue with cold

meant, some backwards photosynthesis
or the science of ghosts, but this was before
cancer melted *his* lungs like blue snowcones

on a heating register, before an embroidered
tree graced the inside of *her* casket, colder
than the gown of Pinnochio's blue fairy.

So I kept quiet one whole winter and the next
not knowing how certain it was
that cold blue had come into my life.

Pi

Fill the unknown with the known.
Is that what we do?

You understand Rome by way of Florence

The angle of a trapezoid
within the arc's hidden curve

Florence by a taxi in Paris

creating a circle of bubbles
trapping fish for food like a circle squared

parts of New York

the bubbles a wall herrings could not cross
circumference a precision

by your own neighborhood.

Archimedes could not cross, a barrier like a puzzle.
This circle filled with known herring

You recognize the prairie

the lunge into ocean, what is not known,
open mouths of whales feeding, bumping

by its coneflower and chicory

crashing back like the answers to pi.
On the blackboard's chalked landscape

sunflowers and loosestrife

or the sea's dark water, between means everything.
This zone could be anything.

the black forest you can see

How our corpus collosums see touch
as safety, milk as love, bridges that span

in a single Douglas fir

an unplumbed realm like a humpback fluking
over waves, leviathans spiraling bubbles into a party

or lone pine cone, tundra and permafrost.

none related, just friends at a barbecue, ritual, tradition.
Or your mother's lavender and smoke perfume

Even though you've never been north

and your father's cologne of sea and tar
instruct who you will love, their smell

of Ohio, you imagine the blizzards

their aroma like bent crayons. Approaching a singularity
you expect the past to show up. It arrives

rimefrost and depth of glaciers

blowing bubbles, smelling like someone's tar
and lavender, with that whiff of Florence

a slow advance like memory.

eyes the color of chicory, hair a coneflower's
center, gestures like the branches of a fir

or the high pierce keening of whales

that voice, the relief of ice after hard sun

filling the Arctic Circle

filling your territory, this corridor

like a rumble.

this alien, this pi, this risk where we live.

*Archimedes discovered pi by filling the circle with every shape's known area. The difference between these and a circle's actual circumference is pi. A singularity is an event that does not fit other phenomena. Humpback whales have been observed in this traditional behavior by Scott Baker and researchers of the Alaska Whale Foundation since 1979. The corpus collosum is where associative memory in the brain develops.

PERIOD

Thank god. Thank the French. Thank everyone.
At last we can escape the tyranny of the comma,

though still use it sparingly. You make our lives
definite. Tell Latin scholars to give it a rest. Stop.

We love you, who really don't see the point. We
would rather take the shortest path in a paragraph.

We love your finality. We love living in the cartouche
of your circle. We love all things contained.

We love you who do not stay out all night. No.
Not ever. We don't want another port and another

rusty nail and another vodka tonic. No. We want it fixed.
We want it in categories. We want each thing to have

its own story. Take this petal of a sunflower. The one
the bee will not be on for twenty more seconds. Yes.

That petal is like a saber. The yellow saber pointed
at your heart. But nothing else. One yellow saber

per heart. That's the way it is. The pause is all. We
like one heartbreak at a time. We like one end.

About the Author

Josie Kearns was born in Flint, Michigan and was raised there by her mother, Gladys Kearns Kibby and her stepfather, Ray Kibby. This is her fourth book of poems and fifth book. The first two, a chapbook by March Street Press and a full-length collection by New Issues Press were both titled *New Numbers*. She has also published a nonfiction book based on lives of laid off autoworkers in new careers, *Life After the Line.* Her next forthcoming book is *Alphabet of the Ocean* from March Street Press. Her work has been awarded four Creative Artist Grants from the Michigan Council for the Arts, three Hopwood Awards, a Cowden Fellowship, a grant to the National Endowment for the Arts in Washington, D.C., a Detroit Women Writers Fellowship and numerous writer-in-residencies from the Ragdale Foundation.

She is the former director of the Visiting Writers Series and Young Writers Academy at the Genesee Literary Center in Flint, Michigan. She currently teaches writing and literature at the University of Michigan in Ann Arbor. Her work has been anthologized in *Boomer Girls, Are You Experienced?*, and *Sweeping Beauty: Women Poets Write About Housework*, all from Iowa University Press, as well as *Contemporary Michigan Poetry: Poems from the Third Coast, Industrial Strength Poetry, Passages North Anthology* and others. Her poems have appeared in journals such as *The Georgia Review, The Iowa Review, Poetry Northwest, Earth's Daughters, The MacGuffin, Moving Out* and others.

Other Recent Titles from Mayapple Press:

Eleanor Lerman, *The Blonde on the Train*, 2008
Paper, 164 pp, $16.95 plus s&h
ISBN 978-0932412-737
Sophia Rivkin, *The Valise*, 2008
Paper, 38 pp, $12.95 plus s&h
ISBN 978-0932412-720
Alice George, *This Must Be the Place*, 2008
Paper, 48 pp, $12.95 plus s&h
ISBN 978-0932412-713
Angela Williams, *Live from the Tiki Lounge*, 2008
Paper, 48 pp, $12.95 plus s&h
ISBN 978-0932412-706
Claire Keyes, *The Question of Rapture*, 2008
Paper, 72 pp, $14.95 plus s&h
ISBN 978-0932412-690
Judith Kerman and Amee Schmidt, eds., *Greenhouse: The First 5 Years of the Rustbelt Roethke Writers' Workshop*, 2008
Paper, 78 pp, $14.95 plus s&h
ISBN 978-0932412-683
Cati Porter, *Seven Floors Up*, 2008
Paper, 66 pp, $14.95 plus s&h
ISBN 978-0932412-676
Rabbi Manes Kogan, *Fables from the Jewish Tradition*, 2008
Paper, 104 pp, $19.95 plus s&h
ISBN 978-0932412-669
Joy Gaines-Friedler, *Like Vapor*, 2008
Paper, 64 pp, $14.95 plus s&h
ISBN 978-0932412-652
Jane Piirto, *Saunas*, 2008
Paper, 100 pp, $15.95 plus s&h
ISBN 978-0932412-645
Joel Thomas Katz, *Away*, 2008
Paper, 42 pp, $12.95 plus s&h
ISBN 978-0932412-638
Tenea D. Johnson, *Starting Friction*, 2008
Paper, 38 pp, $12.95 plus s&h
ISBN 978-0932412-621

For a complete catalog of Mayapple Press publications, please visit our website at *www.mayapplepress.com*. Books can be ordered direct from our website with secure on-line payment using PayPal, or by mail (check or money order). Or order through your local bookseller.